ENDANGERED WILDLIFE
MAMMALS

Anita Ganeri

WAYLAND

CONTENTS

First published in paperback in Great Britain in 2020 by Wayland

Editor: Hayley Fairhead
Design: Elaine Wilkinson

Wayland, an imprint of Hachette Children's Group
Part of Hodder & Stoughton
Carmelite House
50 Victoria Embankment
London EC4Y 0DZ

ISBN: 978 1 5263 0969 3

Printed in Dubai

An Hachette UK Company
www.hachette.co.uk
www.hachettechildrens.co.uk

MIX
Paper from responsible sources
FSC
www.fsc.org
FSC® C104740

Picture credits
Alamy: AvalonPhotoshot 29b; Imagebroker 11t; Mauritius Images GmbH 10-11, 30tcl; Minden Pictures 5t; volkerpreusser 11b.
Nature PL: Karl Ammann 6b; Nigel Bean 4-5; Emanuelle Biggi 1, 12c, 30bc; Mark Cardawine back cover b, 2c, 12b, 16b; Suzi Eszterhas 19; Nick Garbutt 16t, 17t, 30bcr; Laurent Geslin 22b; Steven Kazlowski 21c; Mark MacEwen 13; Vladimir Medvedev 24, 30tcl; Andy Rouse 3c, 7, 9t, 21t; Cyril Ruoso 2t,8, 27t, 30tcr; Roland Seitre back cover t, 22c, 23, 28, 29t , 30cl, 30bl; Anup Shah 3t, 3b, 18t, 18b, 26c, 26b,30cr, 30bcl; Yuro Shibnev 25t; Dave Watts 14, 15t, 30br; Theo Webb 6t, 30tr; Wild Wonders of Europe 20-21, 30tl.
Shutterstock: Chris Humphries: front cover.

Every attempt has been made to clear copyright. Should there be any inadvertent omission, please apply to the publisher for rectification.

MAMMALS IN DANGER

Extinction is when a plant or animal dies out. Scientists think that more than 99 per cent of all the species that have ever lived on Earth are extinct. In the past this was due to massive natural events, such as asteroid strikes. Today, around a quarter of the world's mammals face extinction and it's largely down to humans that their future is so uncertain.

Przewalski's horse came close to extinction, but some were bred in captivity and reintroduced to the wild.

WHAT ARE MAMMALS?

- Vertebrates
- Warm-blooded
- Give birth to live young
- Young feeds on milk provided by its mother
- Often covered in hair.

Under threat

This book looks at some of the most endangered mammals. They have been chosen to show the different threats that they face; from habitat loss or illegal poaching to hunting for their meat or body parts. The good news is that many governments and conservationists are working hard to save these mammals, and their homes, before it is too late.

A polar bear catches a seal to eat as part of an Arctix food chain.

Upsetting the balance

Planet Earth is home to an amazing variety of animals and plants. This variety is known as biodiversity, and it is the result of millions of years of evolution. If animals or plants become extinct, there is a loss of biodiversity. In the natural world, the species in a habitat rely on each other for their survival. For example, in the Arctic, polar bears rely on seals for food, while seals rely on fish. The loss of even one species can have a disastrous knock-on effect.

Danger Rating

The mammals in this book have been given a status rating, set by the IUCN (International Union for the Conservation of Nature). This rating is based on how close to extinction an animal is thought to be. Most of the mammals in this book are critically endangered, endangered or vulnerable. Critically endangered means that they face an extremely high risk of becoming extinct in the wild. Endangered means that they are very likely to become extinct. Vulnerable means that they will probably become endangered unless wthe threats facing them can be reduced.

TIGER

Famous for its stripes, the tiger is one of the largest of the big cats. It lives in forests and mangrove swamps, where its stripes provide camouflage as it stalks its food. A fierce hunter, a tiger has powerful jaws and sharp teeth for killing its prey.

Tigers in trouble

Tigers once roamed large parts of Asia, but in the last 100 years they have lost around 95 per cent of their habitat. The Bali, Javan and Caspian tigers are already extinct. The rest – the Siberian, South China, Sumatran, Indochinese, Malayan and Bengal tigers – are in danger of dying out.

A Bengal tiger will live for eight to ten years in the wild.

Tiger skins, and other animal parts, on sale in Myanmar.

Habitat loss

Habitat loss remains a major threat, as forests are cleared for farmland and homes, while mangrove swamps are being destroyed by flooding and erosion. As their habitat shrinks, and prey becomes harder to find, tigers turn to livestock for food. This puts the tigers in conflict with local farmers. Tigers are also hunted for their skin and bones, which are used in traditional medicine, despite laws banning this trade.

Save the tiger

At the beginning of the twentieth century, there were around 100,000 tigers. A century later, numbers had dropped as low as 3,200. Since then, numbers have risen to around 3,890 thanks to work by conservation groups and governments. In India, for example, Project Tiger works with local people to reduce tiger attacks, and has a Tiger Protection Force to catch poachers. In 2010, project Tx2 was launched by the WWF (World Wide Fund for Nature) in the 13 countries in which tigers are still found. Its aim is to double the number of wild tigers by 2022.

A female Bengal tiger with her cub.

VITAL STATS

Scientific name: *Panthera tigris*

Body length: 2–3 m

Weight: 100–300 kg

Diet: Deer, wild pigs

Numbers in the wild: Around 3,890

Status: Endangered

Location: Asia
(range marked in red below)

Wild fact Tigers are famous for their stripes, but no two tigers have the same stripe pattern. Like human fingerprints, the patterns are all different.

GIANT PANDA

Giant pandas belong to the bear family. They have large, stocky bodies, with striking black and white coats. Once widespread across eastern and southern China, giant pandas now live in a few patches of bamboo forest on remote mountains.

Fussy eater

About 99 per cent of a giant panda's diet is made up of bamboo. The rest is made up of other plants, and even birds and rodents. Bamboo is tough to digest. To get enough nourishment, an adult panda must spend most of its time feeding to eat up to 18 kg of food a day. Pandas use specially adapted wrist bones as thumbs for gripping the bamboo stalks, and pulling them into their mouths.

Habitat destruction

Because pandas rely so much on bamboo, they are very sensitive to changes in their habitat. Bamboo naturally dies back every 20 years or so. In the past, the pandas simply found another patch, but this is no longer possible because of habitat loss. Large areas of forest have been cleared for timber and farming, leaving only small, scattered areas for the pandas.

A panda feeding on its favourite meal of bamboo.

Some pandas are now bred and studied in captivity.

VITAL STATS

Scientific name: *Ailuropoda melanoleuca*

Body length: 150–190 cm

Weight: 70–125 kg

Diet: Mostly bamboo

Numbers in the wild: Around 1,865

Status: Vulnerable

Location: China

Panda protection

Since the 1960s, the giant panda has been the symbol of the WWF. The WWF has been working with the Chinese government and conservation groups to help protect the panda. A captive breeding programme, together with the setting up of special forest reserves, have helped to increase the numbers of pandas in the wild from around 1,000 in the 1970s to around 1,865 today.

Wild fact A giant panda's gut is lined with an extra-thick layer of slimy mucus. This protects the gut from damage that could be caused by sharp splinters of bamboo.

WILD BACTRIAN CAMEL

Superbly adapted to life in the harsh Gobi Desert, wild Bactrian camels can survive for days without drinking, and store fat in their humps for when food is scarce. Their thick fur keeps them warm in the freezing winter, but is shed during the summer heat.

Camel survivors

There may only be around 1,000 wild Bactrian camels left. They are found in four remote locations in north-west China and south-west Mongolia. The largest group lives in part of the Gobi Desert in China.

VITAL STATS

Scientific name: *Camelus ferus*

Height at shoulder: 1.8–2.3 m

Weight: 600–1,000 kg

Diet: Thorny plants and shrubs

Numbers in the wild: fewer than 1,000

Status: Critically endangered

Location: China, Mongolia

Camels at risk

For centuries, wild Bactrian camels have been hunted for their meat and skins. In addition, they are losing their remaining habitat as it is taken over for mining and livestock. Experts estimate a massive 80 per cent drop in their numbers over the next 50 years.

Together with the Wild Camel Protection Foundation, the Chinese and Mongolian governments are working to protect the remaining camels, and two special reserves have been established. A captive breeding programme has also been set up in Mongolia – the only one of its kind in the world.

A herd of wild Bactrian camels in Mongolia.

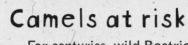

Wild fact

During a sandstorm, a wild Bactrian camel's double row of extra-long eyelashes and long, slit-like nostrils help to keep the sand out of its nose and eyes.

Camels have adapted to survive the arid conditions of the Gobi Desert.

BLACK RHINOCEROS

With its huge, armour-plated body and pointed horns, the black rhino looks like a creature straight out of prehistory. This magnificent animal lives in grasslands, deserts and forests in Africa, where it browses on leaves and woody plants.

Rare rhinos

Once found across large parts of sub-Saharan Africa, black rhinos are now extremely rare. They are mostly found in South Africa, Namibia, Zimbabwe and Kenya. By 1993, black rhino numbers had crashed from around 65,000 to an all-time low of around 2,300 animals. Thanks to conservation efforts, and greater protection, the population has gradually increased to around 5,000.

A black rhino grazing in the Maasai Mara National Park in Kenya.

Guards patrol the parks to protect the rhinos from poachers.

Hunted down

In the past, black rhinos were hunted for their meat and hide. Their habitat was also cleared to make space for farmland and settlements. The main threat that they still face is poaching for their valuable horn. Rhino horn is used in traditional medicine, and for making elaborate handles for ceremonial daggers.

Precious horns

Despite being illegal, the trade in rhino horn continues to grow. Many wild rhinos now live in heavily protected reserves. Some rhinos have their horns deliberately, and painlessly, removed by vets to make the animals worthless to poachers.

VITAL STATS

Scientific name: *Diceros bicornis*

Body length: 3–3.75 m

Weight: 800–1,400 kg

Diet: Leaves, twigs

Numbers in the wild: Around 4,880

Status: Critically endangered

Location: Eastern and Southern Africa

A black rhino that has had its horn removed by vets.

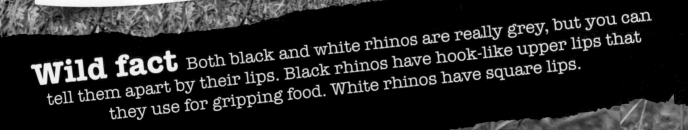

Wild fact Both black and white rhinos are really grey, but you can tell them apart by their lips. Black rhinos have hook-like upper lips that they use for gripping food. White rhinos have square lips.

NORTHERN HAIRY-NOSED WOMBAT

One of the world's rarest mammals, the northern hairy-nosed wombat has a stocky body with silver-grey fur, short, strong legs and a short tail. It uses the strong claws on its front legs like spades for digging burrows where it rests and breeds.

Wild wombats

Today, there are fewer than 200 northern hairy-nosed wombats left in the wild. Their natural habitat is dry grassland and eucalyptus woodland, much of which has been lost to farmland or destroyed by wildfires, floods and droughts. The wombats are also hunted by dingoes, and have found themselves in competition for food with farmers' livestock.

A photo of a northern hairy-nosed wombat in Epping Forest National Park, Australia.

A wombat being released from a trap, after scientists have checked it.

Wombat watch

Most of the surviving wombats live in Epping Forest National Park in Queensland, Australia. To protect them, the park is not open to the public and the wombats are surrounded by a 2-m-high fence to keep predators out. The wombats are closely monitored by rangers and scientists, who use remote cameras to photograph them.

Because there are so few wombats, there is a real danger that a single fire or flood could wipe the whole group and species out. In 2009, several wombats were flown from Epping Forest to the Richard Underwood Nature Refuge to establish another colony, and reduce the risk. The new colony is doing well, with the first baby born in 2017.

VITAL STATS

Scientific name: *Lasiorhinus krefftii*

Body length: More than 1 m

Weight: Around 32 kg

Diet: Grasses

Numbers in the wild: Fewer than 200

Status: Critically endangered

Location: North-east Australia

Wild fact Like kangaroos, wombats are marsupials, with pouches where their babies grow. But the wombat's pouch opens backwards so that it does not fill with earth as it digs its burrow.

AYE-AYE

Found in the forests of Madagascar, the aye-aye is a small mammal with extraordinary looks. It has a thick, grey-brown coat, flecked with white, and a long, bushy tail. Its ears are large and bat-like. It feeds on fruit and insect larvae.

Unlucky lemur

The aye-aye is a type of lemur –Madagascar's best-known animals. Along with 80 per cent of the island's wildlife, the aye-aye is found nowhere else on Earth. Today, it is at serious risk of becoming extinct, as its home is destroyed for timber, and to make space for farming and settlement. Aye-ayes are also killed by local people who believe that they bring bad luck.

An aye-aye at night. The aye-aye's large eyes help it to see in the dark.

Wild fact Aye-ayes have very long, twig-like middle fingers for tapping on tree bark to locate insect larvae. They then tear the bark open with their teeth and scoop the larvae out.

A captive aye-aye with its keeper.

Living alone

The aye-aye is nocturnal, and spends the day sleeping in a twig nest high up in the trees. It is also quite solitary and usually lives on its own. This makes it difficult to monitor, and scientists do not know how many aye-ayes are left in the wild but believe that their numbers are falling fast. Unless their habitat is saved, numbers may drop by half in the next 10–20 years.

Saving the aye-aye

On Madagascar, aye-ayes are protected in several national parks. There are also aye-ayes in zoos around the world, where they form part of captive breeding programmes. Since the 1990s, Jersey Zoo has been working with the government of Madagascar to protect the aye-aye. So far, eight babies have been born at the zoo.

VITAL STATS

Scientific name: *Daubentonia madagascariensis*

Length: (body) 30–40 cm; (tail) 40–50 cm

Weight: 2–3 kg

Diet: Fruit, insect larvae

Numbers in the wild: Not known

Status: Endangered

Location: Madagascar

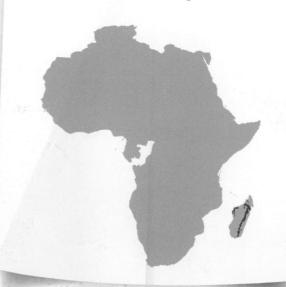

ORANG-UTAN

Orang-utans are large apes, with shaggy, brownish-red fur. Ideally suited for their life in the rainforest, orang-utans have very long arms for swinging through the trees, and hook-shaped hands and feet for gripping branches.

A young male orang-utan uses his long arms to swing about.

On the brink

Once found across south-east Asia, today orang-utans only live on the islands of Borneo and Sumatra, and are close to becoming extinct. There may be as few as 7,500 orang-utans left on Sumatra.

Some orang-utans are killed for meat by hunters, or if they wander into villages. Others, especially young animals, may be captured for the illegal pet trade. But the greatest threat is the loss of the orang-utan's rainforest habitat, which is being cleared for logging, gold mining and palm oil plantations.

Wild fact At night, orang-utans sleep in nests in the trees. They build the nests from bent-over branches and twigs. They add a cover of leaves if it is raining, and use other leaves as pillows.

Nursery care

Orang-utans breed very slowly – females only have one baby about every eight years. This means that even a small fall in numbers could put them at serious risk. The apes are protected by law, and urgent efforts are being made to save their rainforest habitat. Special 'nurseries' have also been set up for orphan orang-utans. Here, they learn skills, such as climbing, that they need in order to return to the forest.

VITAL STATS

Scientific name: *Pongo pygmaeus* (Bornean); *Pongo abelii* (Sumatran)

Body length: 1.3–1.8 m

Weight: 35–80 kg

Diet: Fruit, leaves, shoots

Numbers in the wild: Around 100,000 (Bornean); around 7,500 (Sumatran)

Status: Critically endangered

Location: Sumatra, Borneo

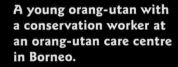

A young orang-utan with a conservation worker at an orang-utan care centre in Borneo.

POLAR BEAR

The largest living land carnivore, a male polar bear can grow up to 2.6 m long and weigh up to 600 kg. It is brilliantly adapted to its freezing Arctic home, with a thick, white fur coat for warmth, strong limbs and large front paws for swimming.

A polar bear hunting on the sea ice in northern Norway.

Seal hunters

The polar bear's favourite prey is ringed seals. It waits by a seal's breathing hole, then pounces when the seal surfaces for air, or hunts them in their icy dens. Using its superb sense of smell, a bear can detect prey a kilometre away, and up to a metre under the ice.

Wild fact To stop them from slipping on the ice, polar bears have sharp claws like ice-picks, and small bumps on the soles of their feet which work like suction cups.

A female polar bear with her cub.

Shrinking ice

Polar bears are found across the Arctic. They live on the ice near the coast where there are plenty of seals to eat. Today, their habitat is under threat from climate change. As the Earth warms, and the sea ice shrinks, the bears are in danger of losing their hunting grounds. This is particularly devastating for pregnant females who need to build up stores of fat to live off when they are nursing their cubs.

Polar bears are superb swimmers.

VITAL STATS

Scientific name: *Ursus maritimus*
Body length: 1.9–2.6 m
Weight: 200–600 kg
Diet: Mostly seals
Numbers in the wild: 20–25,000
Status: Vulnerable
Location: Arctic

Safe haven

If global warming continues at the present rate, it is predicted that the summer sea ice will have disappeared from most of the Arctic by 2040. Only one place may still have ice – the so-called Last Ice Area in Greenland and Canada. Conservationists are planning to protect this region as a rare safe haven for polar bears and other animals.

IBERIAN LYNX

The Iberian lynx is a medium-sized wild cat, with a spotted coat, long legs, a short tail and a small head with long whiskers and tufted ears. It is mainly nocturnal, coming out at dusk to hunt for rabbits to eat.

A female lynx with her cub, which was born in captivity.

Lynx recovery

At the beginning of the twenty-first century, the Iberian lynx was on the verge of extinction, with as few as 90 animals left in the wild. Today, thanks to the hard work of conservationists, their numbers have risen to around 400.

A wild Iberian lynx carrying its rabbit prey.

Rabbit hunters

A skilful hunter, the lynx specialises in catching rabbits, which make up 90 per cent of its diet. Recently, disease wiped out huge numbers of rabbits, meaning that the lynx has had to compete fiercely with other animals for prey. Many lynx are also killed on the roads, or caught in illegal traps set by poachers who hunt them for their fur and meat.

Lynx management

Protected reserves have been set up where conservationists use cameras and radio collars to monitor the lynx. In some places, underground tunnels have been built so that lynx can cross busy roads. Rabbit numbers are carefully managed to make sure that the lynx have enough food. Lynx are also being bred in captivity for reintroduction into the wild.

VITAL STATS

Scientific name: *Lynx pardinus*
Body length: 65–100 cm
Weight: 5–15 kg
Diet: Mostly rabbits
Numbers in the wild: Around 400
Status: Endangered
Location: Portugal, Spain

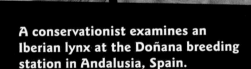

A conservationist examines an Iberian lynx at the Doñana breeding station in Andalusia, Spain.

Wild fact No one is sure why a lynx has hairy ear tufts. The hairs may help to direct sounds into its ears, making it easier for the lynx to locate prey.

AMUR LEOPARD

Found only in two remote forest regions of eastern Russia and north-eastern China, the Amur leopard is one of the rarest big cats. By 2007, numbers had dropped to around 35 leopards. Today, that number has slowly grown to around 70.

Leopard life and death

Amur leopards are nocturnal. During the day, they rest in caves or among thick vegetation, coming out at dawn and dusk to hunt for deer and wild boar. They are well suited to the harsh climate they live in. Their fur coats grow longer and thicker in winter for warmth.

A very rare sighting of a wild Amur leopard in the far east of Russia.

Beautiful fur

Amur leopards were once much more widespread, but were hunted almost to extinction for their beautiful coats, and their bones which are used in traditional medicine. Their habitat has also been destroyed by logging, forest fires and clearance for roads, factories and farms. Today, there are so few left that a large fire could wipe them out.

Scientists fit a radio collar to a leopard to track it.

Leopard rescue

As the leopards' habitat vanishes, so do the animals it preys on, such as deer and wild boar. Conservationists are working to set up protected areas, where the numbers of prey animals can be carefully controlled. They also carry out anti-poaching controls and are helping to train local firefighters to put out deadly forest fires. Many fires are started by local farmers to clear their fields, with devastating results for the leopards.

VITAL STATS

Scientific name:
Panthera pardus orientalis

Length: (body) 107–136 cm; (tail) 82–90 cm

Weight: 25–48 kg

Diet: Deer, wild boar

Numbers in the wild: Around 70

Status: Critically endangered

Location: Russia, China

Wild fact Amur leopards have huge, furry tails which they can wrap around themselves, like scarves, to keep warm.

WESTERN LOWLAND GORILLA

Living in rainforests across West Africa, the western lowland gorilla forms small family groups, made up of an older male, several females and their young. It mostly lives on the ground, but will climb trees to reach fruit and to build a nest to sleep in.

A group of western lowland gorillas, feeding on rotten wood.

Gorilla danger

Over the last 25 years, the number of western lowland gorillas left in the wild has fallen by more than 60 per cent. The main threats facing these apes are habitat loss, poaching and disease. Their forest home is being cleared at an alarming rate to make space for farmland, and this makes it easier for poachers to find and kill the gorillas. Young gorillas are also taken for the illegal pet trade.

A magnificent male gorilla in Sangha Special Dense Forest Reserve in the Central African Republic.

Bushmeat

'Bushmeat' from gorillas is eaten by local people and is highly prized as food and as a source of income. Part of the conservation effort to save the gorillas is to try to find alternatives to bushmeat, such as growing more crops, or raising more fish and livestock.

A vet examines a 5-year-old gorilla at a reintroduction project in Batéké Plateau National Park in Gabon.

VITAL STATS

Scientific name:
Gorilla gorilla gorilla

Body length: 1.2–1.8 m

Weight: 70–180 kg

Diet: Mostly fruit

Numbers in the wild: 100–250,000

Status: Critically endangered

Location: West Africa

Deadly disease

Disease is another serious danger to these gorillas. It is estimated that between 1992 and 2007 around a third of western lowland gorillas were killed by the highly infectious Ebola virus. Scientists are now working on a vaccine that could protect gorillas, and chimps, from this deadly disease.

Wild fact Adult male western gorillas are called silverbacks for the streak of silvery-white hair on their back.

BAIRD'S TAPIR

Baird's tapirs were once found right across Central America. Today, so much of their rainforest habitat has been destroyed that they only survive in a few pockets of forest, and are already extinct across much of their former home.

A Baird's tapir in Belize.

Tapir tracks

Tapirs have barrel-shaped bodies and short legs. Their long, flexible upper lips look like a short version of an elephant's trunk. Tapirs forage for food at night, following well-trodden paths through the undergrowth.

VITAL STATS

Scientific name: *Tapirus bairdii*
Body length: 1.8–2.5 m
Weight: 150–320 kg
Diet: Leaves, seeds, fruit
Numbers in the wild: Unknown
Status: Endangered
Location: Central America

A tapir being cared for at a wildlife rescue centre in Costa Rica.

Skilful swimmers

Good swimmers, tapirs stay close to rivers and streams. They use the water for cooling down on hot days and for hiding from danger.

Tapir threats

The main threat facing Baird's tapirs is loss of their habitat. Huge areas of Central American rainforest have been cleared for cattle ranches, roads and homes. Some tapirs are hunted, while others die from diseases caught from domestic animals brought into the cleared forest.

In most of Central America, tapirs are protected by law, but these laws are often broken. Unless their habitat can be saved, they are at serious risk of dying out. Conservationists are now focusing on managing how logging is carried out. If it is done carefully, and sustainably, leaving patches of habitat behind, there may still be hope for the tapirs.

Wild fact Newborn tapirs have reddish-brown coats with white stripes and spots. These markings help to camouflage them among the dappled light of the forest.

LOCATOR MAP

Giant panda

Polar bear

Wild Bactrian camel

Amur leopard

Tiger

Iberian lynx

Baird's tapir

Western lowland gorilla

Orang-utan

Northern hairy-nosed wombat

Aye-aye

Black rhinoceros

GLOSSARY

Biodiversity The variety of plants and animals that live in the world, or in a particular habitat.

Camouflage The natural colouring, patterns or shape of an animal that help it to blend in with its surroundings.

Captive breeding When endangered animals are bred in captivity, in zoos or wildlife reserves.

Climate change The way in which weather patterns on Earth change over a long period.

Conservationist A person who works to protect and save endangered wildlife and habitats.

Domesticated An animal that has been tamed and is kept as a pet or as a farm animal.

Erosion The way in which the wind and water wear away the landscape.

Evolution The process by which different living things have developed over thousands, or millions, of years.

Extinction When an animal or plant dies out forever.

Global warming A gradual increase in the temperature of the Earth's atmosphere, largely because of human activities, such as burning fossil fuels (oil, gas and coal).

Infectious A disease that can be spread between people or other living things.

Marsupial A mammal with a pouch in which its young develops and grows.

Plantation A large-scale farm that grows crops, such as palm oil, sugar, rubber and coffee.

Poaching Illegally hunting for or catching endangered animals.

Predator An animal that hunts and kills other animals for food.

Species A group of living things with similar features that can breed with each other.

Vaccine A medicine used to protect humans or animals from diseases.

Vertebrate A group of animals that have a backbone.

Warm-blooded Relating to an animal that has a constant body temperature, normally higher than its surroundings.

FURTHER INFORMATION

https://newredlist.iucnredlist.org
The website for the IUCN (International Union for Conservation of Nature) Red List of endangered animals and plants.

www.edgeofexistence.org
A programme set up with the ZSL (Zoological Society of London) to highlight and conserve endangered animals.

www.worldwildlife.org/species
The website of the WWF (World Wide Fund for Nature) with information about endangered animals and conservation projects.

INDEX